ASPIRING AUTHOR SERIES

Workbook Four

Creative

Ways

to
Market and Promote
Your Book

Grace LaJoy Henderson

Workbook Four: Creative Ways to Market and Promote Your Book
Copyright ©2019. Grace LaJoy Henderson
Published by Inspirations by Grace LaJoy
Raymore, MO www.gracelajoy.com

ISBN: 9781073545940

Printed in the United States of America

Table of Contents

A word from the author

I do not consider myself a marketing and promotion expert, per se. However, I designed this workbook to teach marketing and promotion strategies I have used throughout my personal experience, while selling my own books. I have learned, through trial and error, who my particular target audience is and how to sell books to them. I believe that the best thing I can teach aspiring authors is what I have done, and what *has* and *has not* worked for me.

Before we start:

People have a tendency to ask authors, how is your book doing? Well, the *book* is not doing anything, it is only a thing...it can't move. Books do not sale themselves, you must do some things to let the world know that your book is available and that they need your book, and you must also tell them *why* they need your book.

The responsibility for marketing and promotion of your book is totally the job of the author and/or publisher. The author may take on the job themselves or a public relations specialist may be hired to publicize and market the book on the author's behalf. But, either way, the author must be heavily involved in marketing and promoting their book.

1. T   F   A book can move and is able to sell itself.

2. Who is responsible for marketing your book?

3. Who may be hired to publicize and market the book on the author's behalf?

4. The _____ must be heavily involved in _____ and _____ their book.

Name some book marketing and promotion techniques you have used.

1.

2.

3.

4.

5.

Marketing versus Promotion

Marketing activities are geared towards securing book sales from your target audience. *Promotion* activities are geared towards letting your target audience know about your book. While sales may result from promotion, sales are not the expected result of a promotional campaign. Increased exposure of your book to your target audience is the expected result. Marketing usually begins with determining your target audience, which we will discuss under "How to determine your target audience".

Many hours have been spent by many authors *marketing* to the wrong group of people. But on the contrary, people who are not necessarily deemed "target audience" have purchased books just to support the author. Can those people be considered members of the target audience? I think so.

Many hours have been spent on *promotion* with the intention of selling a lot of books. From my personal experience, public relations experts have always told me, "I can't guarantee book sales...nobody can". They could only guarantee that my book would receive a higher level of exposure, causing more people to know about me and my book.

So, if a public relations professional offers to sell a large number of books for a large fee, that may not be a good opportunity for you as a starving author. My belief is this: If a professional is truly able to sale a large number of books, why should they need to collect money up front when they can collect a percentage after they make the promised sales.

The Author – the best sales person

Sometimes, the author is the best person to market and promote their own book. Allowing potential buyers to meet the author is key to a good bookselling campaign. When people become interested in the author, then they want to buy the authors books. For example, when people learn I spent time in foster care and that my mother left and never came back, they become interested in reading the book I wrote about my foster care story, A Gifted Child in Foster Care: A Story of Resilience. Then, when they learned that I recently found my mother after five decades, they were even more interested in reading my foster care story.

When people are able to meet me as a part of my book promotion, then marketing becomes easier. For example, when I walk into a school with book samples and post cards about the books, the school is more likely to make a purchase than if I just mail the post card or just call the school. Also, if I am able to do an author presentation, in conjunction with a book purchase, schools are more likely to add my books to their classrooms and libraries. But, not to mention, the books they purchase need to be a good fit with their instructional goals for the school year.

So, they may meet me, but if my book is not a good fit with their current curriculum goals, then they will not buy it. This is another reason why it is important to be sure your time is spent promoting to the correct target audience.

In-person guest author presentations may include:

- Reading a poem you wrote
- Reading an excerpt from your book
- Sharing helpful information
- Giving an inspirational speech
- Conducting a book signing
- Facilitating a workshop
- Purchasing an exhibit table at an event

When I conduct in-person guest author presentations, attendees are more likely to want to purchase autographed copies of my books after the presentation. Besides walk-in visits and setting appointments to meet with my target audience, in-person presentations result in the most book sales.

When should marketing and promotion begin?

Marketing begins at the very thought of writing your book and continues throughout the writing, producing and publishing stage. For example, when you begin to think about what you want to write about, you must think about who will want to read your story. Most importantly you must think about who will actually <u>buy</u> your story. Thus, you must begin thinking about your "target audience". This is done by taking the time to Determine Your WHO (which is outlined in Step #2 in Workbook One of the Aspiring Author Series, 4 Steps to Begin Writing Your Book). Ask yourself these questions:

- Who is your audience?
- Who do you want to read your book?
- Who will benefit from the information in your book?
- Who will care about the information in your book?

Your responses to these questions (Your WHO) should be included during the process of:

- Determining your book title and subtitle
- Creating your cover art
- Writing your back cover description, and
- Creating your Author Bio

Authors should know who their target audience is and attempt to understand the needs of their target audience before beginning the writing process. However, many aspiring authors feel passionate about the subject they want to write about before knowing WHO their target audience will be. Yet, it is still important to try to pinpoint, as soon as possible, a group of people who will be most likely to make a purchase of your book.

You should try to have an idea of who your target audience will be while you are considering all of the things that will attract buyers to your book. For example, your Author Bio establishes your credentials to write about your chosen topic. When readers have faith in the author, they are likely to buy the book, which goes back to the idea of the author being the best sales person.

While marketing may begin while you are creating your book, promotion may begin immediately after the book is complete, and continue until the official publication date. *Note: The time between the completion of the book and the official publication date is the prepublication period. Promotion done during this period is called Early Promotion, and is discussed under the "How to use Marketing and Promotion Strategies to sell more books".* Since books are complete and available for sale at this time, some marketing can take place during the prepublication period. Both marketing and promotion may continue after publication of the book.

How to determine your target audience.

What is a target audience?

A target audience...

- is interested in your book
- cares about your book
- wants to read your book
- desires to share your book with others
- benefits in some way from your book
- has the money to buy your book
- is willing to spend the money they have to purchase buy your book

A true target audience is not only interested in your book, but they actually *have the money to buy your book*, but it does not stop there. A true target audience is also *willing to spend their money on your book*. Furthermore, your target audience should have a reason to share the news about your book with others, buy additional copies of it for others, and encourage others to do the same. A strong target audience has a natural way of attracting other people just like themselves to your book. Facebook Advertising calls this a Look-a-like audience.

How I determined the target audience for my books

Most of the books I have written were written out of inspiration, so I did not necessarily determine a target audience in advance of publishing many of my books. As a result, it was difficult to pinpoint a target audience after the fact. But, enough readers have expressed an interest in, and an appreciation for, my writing for me to feel confident that my work had not been in vain.

Every book I have written has allowed me to fulfill my passion as well as to share inspirational, encouraging and educational things that I desired in my heart to share. My thought is this: If <u>one</u> person is inspired, encouraged, or learns something from something I published, then my mission has been accomplished.

So, I guess what I am saying is that book writing and publishing is not *always* about money. But, if your goal is to sell books and make money, then determining your target audience in advance will be vital.

I determined my target audience in advance for my book for aspiring authors, *Writer's Breakthrough: Steps to Copyright and Publish Your Own Book* and my foster care story, *A Gifted Child in Foster Care: A Story of Resilience.* I also determined my target audience for my latest children's books series in advance of publication. I have also spent more time and money on marketing and promotion for these books. As a result, these titles have been my best sellers.

Here is an example: For the *Writer's Breakthrough* book, I targeted writers who desired to publish their own book, but did not know where to begin. I did two things during publication, to prepare to promote my book to this particular audience: I subtitled the book, *Steps to Copyright and Publish Your Own Book;* and I also added a tagline to the front cover which reads, *Educating Writers Who Know Nothing About Book Publishing.* These simple, yet descriptive messages let my target audience know, just by reading the front cover, that this book is designed specifically to offer help to them.

How did I determine the target audience for the Writer's Breakthrough book? Well, after I published my very first book, *More Than Mere Words: Poetry That Ministers,* I created a 2-page list of steps I had taken to publish the book. I had this list of steps available during my first book signing for the book. Then, I expounded on the steps to teach "How to publish your book" as a 16-week class at a local Bible college.

A lot of people asked me how I wrote my first book. A lot of people also thanked me for sharing my researched information that they had not been able to secure from any other source. This let me know that there was a real, and very large, audience in need of the book publishing information I had assembled.

How I located my target audience for my books

Locating my target audience for *Writer's Breakthrough, A Gifted Child in Foster Care*, and *The Gracie Series* was different for each of these three publications.

Writer's Breakthrough

I located my target audience for *Writer's Breakthrough* in several ways: People who purchased my poetry book and wanted to more information about the steps I took to published the book; People who wanted to publish a book who needed the information; Referrals from people who had been helped by the information; Word of mouth from people who knew someone who wanted to publish a book; People who attended my free Writer's Breakthrough workshops that I held annually for nine years; People who attended my mini workshops at churches and libraries; People who purchased book publishing consultations from me; and aspiring authors who I provided free book publishing consultations for.

Because of the natural demand for this information, my targeted audience found me without a lot of effort on my part, which has made it easy for me to promote and market to this particular audience.

A Gifted Child in Foster Care

As for my foster care story, *A Gifted Child in Foster Care: A Story of Resilience*, I located my target audience in a different way. Whereas, Writer's Breakthrough is educational, my foster care story is inspirational. I located my target audience by requesting testimonials from executives in youth services fields such as directors of foster care and adoption agencies, children's shelters, children and family services, as well as school district administrators.

Obtaining these testimonials was also a marketing and promotion tool that I initiated during the publishing process. In addition to creating an attractive title and subtitle, I incorporated the back cover testimonies from professionals in the field to attract more members of my target audience. One benefit of the testimonials was that those who provided testimonials were introduced to the book, which gave them an opportunity to consider actually making a purchase for their organizations.

Ultimately, the target audience for this book ended up being: People who attended events and conferences where I was the speaker, sharing my foster care story (the attendees purchased my book after my presentation); Conference leaders who purchased my book in advance of the conference, so I could autograph them for everyone who attended the conference; and schools.

Eventually, schools became my largest target audience. Here is how that came about: Two years after publishing the book, *A Gifted Child in Foster Care*, I wanted to market and promote it more widely to schools. So, since the reading level of the book was 4th grade, I studied the Missouri General Learning Expectations (GLEs) for 4th through 7th grade. I used this information to create a student workbook and a matching teacher's guide that promotes reading comprehension skills and character education. These two new additions were beneficial to make the new "classroom set" attractive to educators for classroom use.

By studying the Missouri GLEs, I was preparing to meet a need for 4th through 7th grade students in Missouri public schools. As a result, upper elementary and middle schools (my target audience) were able to use district funds to purchase the classroom set.

The Gracie Series

As for *The Gracie Series*, I was thinking of marketing and promoting to schools as I was creating the series. One of the things I did to prepare while creating the books for the series was to create discussion questions in the back of each book to help elementary classroom teachers engage their students in discussion without a lot of effort on their part. Other things I did were:

- Added matching logos to each book
- Placed logo in same spot on each book cover
- Used matching font for each book title
- Published an overall description of the series on the opening page of each book
- Placed all details in same spot on each book (i.e. book description and about the author)

In addition, I chose the best quality ink for printing. I was tempted to use less quality ink to save money on the cost of printing each book, but I realized that if customers received high quality books, they would be more likely to recommend *The Gracie Series* to other possible buyers. To attract the largest number of buyers, I offered the books in paperback, hardcover and e-book.

Besides just doing things, during the writing of the books, that would attract my target audience, I had no other plans on doing heavy marketing and promoting after the series was published. But, after the completion of the books, and before the official publication date, my target audience began to notice the books just from word-of-mouth (pre-publication buyers sharing their testimonies about the books with people who they knew). My target audience also began to notice the books from me naturally sharing my own excitement about *The Gracie Series* on and off social media.

During this natural demand period, one retired school principal noticed the impact *The Gracie Series* could make in local elementary schools. She knew there was a current need, as well as available funding, in school districts for these books. So, she invited me to an event for educators who all had doctorate degrees, provided me with a free exhibitor table and encouraged me to market and promote *The Gracie Series* to them.

As a result, over half of the books on my table sold out before the event began. There were no sets left by the end of the event. In addition, several of the educators gave me their contact information and asked me to call them at their various schools and districts so they could order more of the books. This is the moment when I knew the importance of pursuing my target market more heavily than I had originally planned.

After this natural demand period, to attract more attention from my target audience, I did the following things:

- Asked for referrals from purchasers
- Sent postcards
- Sent emails
- Attended exhibits
- Purchased Facebook Ads
- Created a video for the Series
- Created a video for each book

All of these things resulted in inquiries, sales and invitations provide presentations.

How to make your book more available to potential buyers.

Some ways to make your book more available are:

- Radio appearances
- Radio commercials
- Television appearances
- Television commercials
- Newspaper articles
- Newspaper advertisements
- Book reviews
- Press Releases

The promotion avenues listed above garnered additional attention for myself and my books, but, not necessarily more book sales. If you search for Grace LaJoy online, a lot of information comes up, which is a direct result of these, and other types of promotion over the years.

Radio appearances. I have been guest on numerous radio shows, both offline and online. Whenever I have been a guest on radio shows, the interview was coupled with book giveaways to listeners who call in, and/or sharing information that the radio audience may be interested in. That information may include, but not be limited to, sharing education or inspirational material, announcing an upcoming event that I will be attending or hosting, sharing what inspired me to begin writing books, sharing my foster care story or simply sharing a poem.

Radio commercials. I have purchased numerous radio commercials. Usually, the radio station ask me to write a script within the allowable seconds or minutes. Then the station uses their voice to read it and sometimes adds music to the background. In most cases, the radio station asked me to provide copies of the promoted book for free giveaway during the promotion period. Also, in most cases, the promotion that I purchased included an author radio interview.

Television appearances. I have made several television appearances, including Fox 4 News and TBN. On Fox 4 News, I discussed my very first book, More Than Mere Words: Poetry That Ministers! On TBN, I discussed my book, Sexual Purity and the Young Woman. As a self-published author, it not always easy to secure television appearances. I got the Fox 4 News appearance because I knew a lady who worked at the station. She talked to the news anchor and set up the interview. I got the TBN interview when I met a television pastor who hosted a show on the channel.

Television Commercials. In addition to the two television appearances, I appeared on several cable channels through an infomercial I created for my *More Than Mere Words: Poetry That Ministers!* poetry book. In this infomercial, I was interviewed and several readers offered real, genuine testimonials about the book. Also, a clip of the famous author and motivational speaker Les Brown was played, in which he said some inspiring words about the book and one of the poems from the book entitled, *I Forgive You.*

Newspaper articles. I have been featured with my books in numerous newspaper articles; local, regional and national; online and offline. For those articles, an interviewer usually sets up an appointment with me to talk about myself and my books. Then s/he develops an intriguing story to be printed in the newspaper. The articles usually garnered attention from people who knew me and people who did not. The people who knew me shared the article with others, and told me they saw my story in the newspaper. People who read the article, who did not know me, now knew something about me.

Newspaper advertisements. I have also paid for newspaper advertisements in several local papers. I chose local newspapers for several reasons. One being it was more affordable. But, mostly I learned early on that marketing and promotion should always begin in the place where the author is known and spread outward from there as popularity picks up.

Book Reviews. I sent my first two books out to numerous major book review outlets, like Midwest Book Review and Kirkus. I also solicited book reviews from newspapers and magazines editors. After the first two books, I stopped mailing out copies requesting reviews because it felt like too much work. I spent too much time mailing out tens of books to end up with only minimal book reviews. The outcome was not worth the time spent for me. For my most recent publications, *The Gracie Series*, I learned the importance of receiving book reviews from readers on Amazon.

Press Releases. Press Releases are designed to tell a story about, or be related to, your book. It should not sound like a sales ad. I have written and published many press releases, and they have garnered a lot of exposure. However, only one press release I published actually resulted in a lot of book sales. It was the press release in which I reported finding my mother after 50 years. As a subtle marketing strategy, I briefly mentioned the book and placed a link to it in the press release.

The press release title was *Kansas City Woman Reunites With Her Long Lost Mother After 50 Years.* It was published through BlackNews.com and shared on their Facebook page. Hundreds of people liked, shared and commented on it. The majority of the comments were congratulating me for finally finding my mother, and from people whose hearts were genuinely pricked from reading my story. As a result, book sales for my foster care story, *A Gifted Child in Foster Care: A Story of Resilience* increased during the distribution of this particular press release.

Why did this press release result in more book sales than past press releases? The press release was a true story of hope and it made people feel inspired. It gave many people confidence that they, too, could possibly find a long-lost loved one.

How to use online tools to help more readers learn about your book.

Since the bulk of my online experience has been on Facebook, I will focus on my Facebook marketing and promotion. I will discuss how I promote my books on my personal page, my author page, and in book promotion groups. Then, I will discuss the book promotion group that I created, and how I use *Facebook Ads* to market my books. Lastly, I will provide some tips on how to market and promote respectfully on Facebook.

Personal Page: Share only natural, non-soliciting, non-marketing things. Briefly share about an author event you attended or a book signing you had. If possible "share" this information from your author page, which we talk about next, as oppose to actually posting it on your personal page. Do not blatantly promote to your Facebook friends though this page. Let your personal page be personal.

Author Page: Ask your friends from your personal page to "like" your author page. Start by asking only your friends who you *know* would be interested in your author page...those who you feel are your greatest supporters. Facebook may block you from inviting friends if it appears you are just going through your friend list inviting everyone. So, invite those who you truly feel would be interested in your work.

Book Promotion Groups: Ask to join groups that perfectly match the content of your book; and that perfectly match your intention. For example, if you want to promote, only join groups that clearly allow promotion within the group.

My book promotion group. I created a group on Facebook called, *Promote Your Book.* I clearly laid out exactly what type of books may be promoted in the group. However, people with all kinds of books, outside of my clearly set requirement, have asked to join the group. I usually delete their request with no explanation, since I have already explained the requirements my introduction of the group.

Furthermore, some people will initially answer the screening questions based on the answer I am looking for, just to get accepted into the group. But as soon as they get accepted, they post a about a book that totally goes against the guidelines of the group. I usually delete their request to post their book. But, I don't necessarily delete the person. However, if they continually attempt to post unrelated things in the group, then I will delete the person from the group. Also, if someone tries to promote anything that is not clearly a book, then I will delete their post. By the way, I fixed my settings for the group so that I must approve all requests to join, as well as all posts.

Some Facebook groups let people join and post without monitoring. But, I monitor because I'd rather have just a handful of people in my group that fit the description of the group, than to compromise and have a group that does not fit the vision I have for the group.

I have joined numerous Facebook groups and, at one time, I was consistently posting in all of the groups. But, one day Facebook blocked me from posting for a limited period of time. After that experience, I chose to continue posting only in the groups that most closely fit my book content. Even though the groups I posted in were specifically "book promotion" groups and the group administrator encouraged book promotion in the group, Facebook had a problem with group members posting too much in these groups. So, I was blocked again. As a result, I stopped posting so much at one time and began to spread my posts out, with hopes Facebook would not block me again. But, yet and still, I was blocked again. So, since Facebook does not make their rules and guidelines about posting in groups clear, I never knew exactly when posting in groups would result in blockage.

So, I don't post in groups to that magnitude anymore. However, when I was able to post in all of those groups (without getting blocked by Facebook) I gained a lot of traffic to my author pages, videos and downloads of my free books on Amazon. So, posting in groups was advantageous, but I believe Facebook wanted to put a stop to it in order to encourage people like myself to purchase more of their paid advertisement. But, I do still post in book promotion groups periodically. I just don't go overboard and I try not to post in too many groups in one day.

Whereas, I used to post in 30 to 50 groups at one time, now I post in less than 10 groups at one time. And whereas, I use to post in groups almost every day, I now only post in groups maybe one time per month.

Facebook Advertising: Whenever I place an ad on Facebook, I usually target "Friends and Friends of Friends". I believe that people who already know me, who are familiar with my work, and who already like it, are more likely to show interest by sharing my ads with their friends and family, more so than someone on Facebook who may have never heard of me or my work.

It has been said that people have to see one ad 7 times before they take some type of action in response to it. A lot of my friends have said "I will buy one day" and they have shared my promotions with their friends. So, I want them to see my ad 6 more times; as opposed to choosing a new audience, who may not be familiar with me or my books. It seems advantages for me to market to the same group (people who have already heard of me) over and over, instead of to switching up my audience.

I would rather be a household name for 10 people than just a passerby for 100 people. The 10 who love my books will provide word of mouth to others and I will reach another 100 or more that way; and they will not just be a passersby audience. They will actually be a focused audience who have a genuine interest, who in turn may provide even more word of mouth for my books.

To market and promote respectfully on Facebook, do not post promotions to your friends' inbox or their page without first asking their permission. Do not tag your friends in images and promotions that do not concern them or when there is no legitimate reason for them to be tagged (i.e. neither they, nor anyone one they know personally, are shown in an image). Only share your promotions with people who have shown an interest and who you know will happily welcome your marketing and promotional energies.

To reach more people in a respectful way, use Facebook ads. If you are reluctant to invest in Facebook ads, keep this in mind: If you participate in the things I have cautioned you not to do, people may hide, unfollow, report or block you and your posts. But, if you do things in a respectful manner, there is a higher chance that your friends will see more of your posts, especially when you post them in acceptable places, like on your own page. When you post respectfully, you can rest assured that if someone wants to share your promotion with their friends, they will.

Book Promotion versus Book Sales

Should an author pay someone a lot of money to help sell tons of books? Is it worth the investment? Can someone guarantee book sales? I believe that if someone could really help sell tons of books, then they would not need a large amount of money up front. If they could guarantee book sales, they would be confident enough to sell the books first, then get a percentage of every book sale.

Book Promotion involves providing exposure through placing information about your book in places where more potential buyers may learn about it. **Book Sales** may, or may not, occur when more people learn about your book. If the group of people who your book is being promoted to is a true target audience, as described on Page 11, then resulting book sales will absolutely occur. The challenge is in finding a true authentic target audience to promote to.

Book Promotion may cause you to become well known, but you may not necessarily have any **Book Sales** or money to show for your popularity. For example, let's look at a childhood star who is now an adult: A young man who played on a well-known television sitcom was "job-shamed" for working at a local market 25 years after he became well-known as a television star. The popular sitcom gave him *promotion*, but not enough money to be financially secure after the show ended.

How to use Marketing and Promotion Strategies to sell more books

The marketing strategies that have worked best for me has been Word of Mouth, Free Promotions, Discounts and Early Promotions. Whatever strategies I use, I believe in true sincere promotions, which I explain at the end of this section.

Word of mouth. This happens when people naturally talk about your book to other people. We encourage word of mouth for our books when we share ourselves, and our work, with others without soliciting; without making people feel like we want something from them; without the causing them to feel pressure to buy; without being pushy or blatantly promoting (i.e. free download of a book). We also encourage word of mouth when we offer people information, education, encouragement and inspiration without asking for anything in return (i.e. free workshop). When we sincerely serve people, they are more likely to talk about it to others, thus spreading word of mouth. Finally, we encourage word of mouth when we genuinely have a good book and people genuinely like us as an author.

Free promotions. Free should always be free! with no stipulations or conditions...no strings attached. If there are stipulations or conditions then what you are giving is not truly free. Maybe you want something from the people to whom you are offering something free, but they should not be required to give you what it is you want. Maybe you hope they will purchase something from you in return, but it should not be a requirement and they should in no way be made to feel obligated to buy; nor should they be made to feel guilty if they do not. They should feel free to accept what you are offering with absolutely no pressure to give anything in return. If they are required to provide their name, email address, phone number, or etc. so that you may promote to them in the future, then what you are offering is not "free". It is okay if it is not free, but just be sure to let the potential buyer know all of the details up front so they will make an educated decision about whether they want to accept your "free" product or service.

Example of a Free Promotion: During my free Writer's Breakthrough workshops, attendees receive information with an opportunity, not an obligation, to buy books. They are free to leave at the end of the workshop without purchasing anything. Yes, I want to gain something; I hope to sell books, but, there was no requirement for them to buy. The workshop was absolutely free. But, some attendees truly wanted my books after the workshop and so I have them available to those who genuinely want to make a purchase.

In addition, during my free Writer's Breakthrough workshop, I give away free books at my book table. This encourages attendees to visit my book table and take a look at the items I have for sale. But, they still are not required to buy anything.

On the other hand, I conduct a free drawing for prizes. But, I don't consider it totally free because attendees must fill out an entry questionnaire to be entered into the free drawing. But, I make the requirement clear to the attendees in advance. So, they are able to make an educated decision about accepting their "free" entry into the drawing.

Another Example of a Free Promotion: I give away the first book in The Gracie Series, Popcorn Behind the Bush, absolutely free. The hope is that those who download it would learn about, become interested in, and subsequently make a purchase of other books in the series. The hope is also that free downloads will result in word of mouth and online reviews of the free eBook

Discounts. Discounts are when an author offers to sell their books for a price lower than they usually sell them for, as an attempt to sell more books.

Example of Discounts: A marketing tool that has been a win-win over and over again is one for $13 or two for $20. This is when I sell one book for $13, but when the buyer purchases two, then both books cost a total of $20, which gives the buyer a savings of $6. This is a win-win for both the buyer and myself. If I sell one book my profit per book is higher than if I sell two books. But, my total profit is still more than if I had sold only one book. Some authors may see this as a loss for the author. But, in reality, many buyers who only intended to buy one book end up buying an additional book, since the discount makes it more affordable for them to buy two.

Another Example of Discounts: Offering classroom sets include creating a set of books to accommodate a classroom of students. When schools purchase the classroom set, they save a significant amount of money per book than if they purchase single copies of a book. The classroom set for my Gifted Child in Foster Care includes 20 books, 20 student workbooks, and 1 teacher's guide. The classroom set for The Gracie Series includes 20 each of 6 books for a total of 120 books.

Early promotion. We already discussed "When should marketing and promotion begin?" But, we are bringing it up again just to say this: Marketing during the writing of your book is a *marketing strategy*. When you incorporate the needs and desires of your target audience when creating your title, subtitle, front and back covers, and author bio, you are indeed integrating a marketing strategy in advance of introducing your book to the public.

Marketing and promotion to the *public* should begin about four months before the official publication date of your book. The best way to accomplish this is to first complete your book. Then set your official publication date for the book for four months away. Since the book is technically complete, you may begin spreading the word to, and soliciting sales from, family and friends. You may also begin requesting interview and book reviews from news sources, like radio, television, papers and magazines. It is a good idea to start with local sources.

Sometimes authors jump right in to try to become famous and nationally known. But, it is best to start with the people you already know and with the sources you already have a natural relationship with. If your natural sources happen to be national, then that is okay. But begin your market and promotion by doing what comes natural.

Another thing you may do during this four-month period is mail and pass out postcards, flyers and emails, to introduce your book and offer prepublication discounts.

Activity

Write your mission, vision and/or purpose for marketing and promoting your book.

Final Question

Name 5 of the techniques you learned from this book that you plan to use for your own book marketing and promoting.

1.

2.

3.

4.

5.

Notes:

_____

_____

_____

_____

_____

_____

_____

_____

_____

_____

_____

_____

_____

_____

_____

Notes:

_____

_____

_____

_____

_____

_____

_____

_____

_____

_____

_____

_____

_____

_____

Notes:

_____

_____

_____

_____

_____

_____

_____

_____

_____

_____

_____

_____

_____

_____

ASPIRING AUTHOR SERIES WORKBOOK DESCRIPTIONS

Available in eBook and softcover at Amazon

ASPIRING AUTHOR SERIES

Workbook One

4

Steps

to
Begin Writing Your Book

Grace LaJoy Henderson

o you have a book inside of you, but, do not know how to put it onto
per? This simple workbook is designed to help you finally get your
ok out of your head and onto paper! This workbook will provide
u with a foundation on which to begin, and to build upon, your new
ok idea.

ASPIRING AUTHOR SERIES

Workbook Two

Steps

to
Producing Your Book

Grace LaJoy Henderson

Do you have a book written, but need help formatting it into
professional product? What should the front cover look like? Wh
information should be included on the back cover and inside page
Learn the steps to producing your book from an experienced auth
and become motivated to complete your book!

ASPIRING AUTHOR SERIES

Workbook Three
Quiz Workbook

Steps

to
Publishing Your
Own Book

Grace LaJoy Henderson

Do you desire to publish your own book, but do not know where to begin? This **Quiz Workbook**, in conjunction with *Writer's Breakthrough: Steps to Copyright and Publish Your Own Book*, teaches the steps necessary to produce, copyright and publish your own book. Get the information you need to make your book available to the world!

Note: This book should only be used together with the Writer's Breakthrough book.

ASPIRING AUTHOR SERIES

Workbook Four

Creative Ways

to
Market and Promote
Your Book

Grace LaJoy Henderson

Have you published your book, but need insight on how to mark
and promote it? This book provides tips to help you determine you
target market and make your book more available to potential buyer
Learn how to use online and offline tools to help more readers lear
about your book; and the best avenues to secure book sales. Learn th
best time to begin promoting your book, which may be earlier tha
you think!

www.ingramcontent.com/pod-product-compliance
Lightning Source LLC
Chambersburg PA
CBHW072303170526
45158CB00003BA/1162